WILHELM RICHARD
WAGNER

Richard Tames

Franklin Watts
London • New York • Sydney • Toronto

Contents

False Starts	**4**
Schopenhauer	**9**
Success and Exile	**10**
Ludwig II of Bavaria	**18**
A Royal Rescue	**19**
The Ring	**25**
Last Years and Legacy	**26**
Find Out More ...	**30**
Glossary	**31**
Index	**32**

© Franklin Watts 1991

First published in Great Britain
in 1991 by
Franklin Watts
96 Leonard Street
London EC2A 4RH

First published in the USA by
Franklin Watts, Inc.
387 Park Avenue South
New York, N.Y. 10016

First published in Australia by
Franklin Watts
14 Mars Road
Lane Cove
NSW 2066

UK ISBN: 0 7496 0479 4

Phototypeset by: JB Type, Hove, East Sussex
Printed in: Belgium
Series Editor: Hazel Poole
Designed by: Nick Cannan

A CIP catalogue record for this book is available from the British Library.

False Starts

Almost everything about Richard Wagner is controversial — even the question of his birth. He was the ninth child of Johanna, wife of Karl Friedrich Wilhelm Wagner. It was long suspected, however, that Richard's real father was the actor, Ludwig Geyer, a family friend who later became his stepfather. Wagner himself encouraged this belief and from the age of nine until he was 15 used Geyer's surname as his own. It was also believed that Johanna, Wagner's mother, was the illegitimate daughter of Prince Constantin, the brother of the Grand Duke of Weimar. In 1986, over a hundred years after Wagner's death, it was finally discovered that Johanna was *not* the daughter of Constantin, but his mistress, and that, therefore, Wagner's suspected grandfather was, in fact, his real father. Uncertain about his origins, the composer was to be certain only about his destiny — to be a genius.

Wilhelm Richard Wagner was born at Leipzig, a city famed for music, on 22 May 1813. His supposed father, Karl Friedrich, was a respected police official who died of typhus six months after the baby's birth. Less than a year later Johanna, left with a large family to bring up, married Ludwig Geyer, bearing him a daughter seven months later.

The whole Geyer-Wagner family had a passionate interest in the theatre. Even Karl-Friedrich had been an amateur actor. Geyer himself was not only an actor but also a writer and painter. Richard's brother, Albert, became a successful **tenor** while his sister Rosalie made her name as an actress, and two other sisters became opera singers.

Richard himself appeared for the first time on stage (as an angel) while still a small child and took piano lessons from the age of seven, though he preferred to play by ear rather than learn through formal training. He never became a good pianist and later failed to master the violin. It was the same story at school, where he developed a passionate interest in Greek **myths** but hated the tedious task of mastering Greek grammar. All through his life he was willing to drive himself like a slave, but only at what interested him and in the way he wanted to. At the age of 15 he played truant from school for six months (unknown to his mother) so that he could work on a tragedy in the style of Shakespeare. The resulting *Leubald and Adelaide* had over 40 characters but the young dramatist killed so many of them off in the course of the plot that he had to bring some of them back in the last act as ghosts to be able to finish the play.

Wagner's addiction to opera began when he was a small child, when Geyer took him to see a performance of a work by Weber, a friend of

Family likeness? Wagner's mother Johanna (left), **brother, Albert** (who became a successful tenor) **and half-sister, Cecilie Geyer.**

Geyer's and conductor of the Saxon court orchestra. The boy's devotion was confirmed after he heard the famous soprano Wilhelmine Schröder-Devrient sing in Beethoven's *Fidelio*. He decided that he must study music to add that element to his play.

In 1828, Wagner began to study musical composition seriously, and his first efforts at composing included a string quartet, a piano sonata, several concert overtures and a symphony. On Christmas Day 1830, when he was 17, one of his overtures was performed in public at a charity concert, but it was badly scored and both the orchestra and the audience seem to regard it as little more than a crude effort by a self-taught boy. Undeterred, Wagner decided that he could, after all, benefit from some formal training and was taken on by C.T. Weinlig, who also taught Schumann and was successor to Bach as **cantor** of St. Thomas's Church in Leipzig. Weinlig managed to

Leipzig, the musical city which produced Bach, Schumann and Mendelssohn.

interest his pupil in the technical discipline of composition, but Wagner also continued with his own scheme of self-education, studying every Beethoven score he could get hold of and going to as many different operas as he could.

In 1831, Wagner was accepted as a music student at the University of Leipzig, which demanded lower qualifications for music than most other courses. He enjoyed drinking, duelling, gambling and chasing girls, paid little attention to his studies, and got into debt. He then visited Vienna and ran up even more debts. Returning through Prague he was fortunate to have his symphony performed by the students of the Conservatory. But he was not so lucky with his first attempt at an opera. His sister Rosalie said it would be impossible to perform and so he destroyed it.

In 1833, thanks to his brother, Albert, Wagner got a job at the Würzburg theatre as a chorusmaster, which involved drilling the cast (apart from the lead singers) through their parts. It was dull work and lasted only a year, but it enabled him to evade military service in Saxony, helped him to learn the popular operas of his day and gave him time to write his second opera, *Die Feen (The Fairies)*. Failing to interest anyone in it, he then wrote another, *Das*

Minna, a talented opera singer who became Wagner's long-suffering wife.

Liebesverbot (The Ban on Love), based on Shakespeare's *Measure for Measure*.

Wagner's next job was as a conductor with a rundown touring company based in Magdeburg. He nearly didn't accept the offer, but changed his mind when he saw the company's leading actress, Christine Wilhelmine (Minna) Planer, whom he found "very charming and fresh in appearance." She was not particularly clever, she was older than him and she had an illegitimate daughter of six (whom she passed off as her younger sister), but she was a competent actress who left the company shortly afterwards to seek work in Königsberg.

Despite his lack of experience Wagner quickly became a successful conductor, popular with performers and audiences alike. He stayed at Magdeburg long enough to see a bad production of *Das Liebesverbot*, which ended in disaster and a fistfight among the artists at the second performance. Shortly afterwards, the company went bankrupt and was disbanded.

Wagner then followed Minna to

Königsberg, where they were married in November 1836. She was loyal, kindly and remarkably forgiving, but she was not suited for the almost impossible demands Wagner would make of her. In May 1837, convinced that she had made a disastrous choice of husband, Minna fled to her parents in Dresden. Wagner followed, they were reconciled, and then Minna fled again.

Wagner next found a job in Riga, a trading city on the Baltic coast, where Minna rejoined him accompanied by her sister Amalie, whom Wagner had hired as a singer. Throughout 1838, Wagner worked on his next project, *Rienzi*, a spectacular opera in the style of Meyerbeer, the king of Parisian music. The story itself, about a medieval Italian adventurer, was based on an historical romance by the English novelist, Bulwer-Lytton.

In March 1839, Wagner was told that his contract would not be renewed. He and Minna had now run up large debts. A return to Germany would be difficult, as they had left unpaid bills there as well. Wagner decided that they should go to Paris. To finance the trip they sold Minna's stage costumes and even their furniture, but there was still the problem of getting there. Paris was a long way away and their passports were being held by their creditors. Telling everyone that they were going on a trip to the countryside, they slipped out of Riga and made their way by backroads and forest paths to the border, where they dashed across while the frontier guards were changing shifts. Making their way to the Prussian port of Pillau, they hid until they could board the *Thetis,* like stowaways, by night. The voyage should have taken eight days. In fact bad weather prolonged it to more than three weeks and landed them thoroughly shaken and bedraggled, not in France but in London.

Giacomo Meyerbeer (1791-1864), pianist and composer whose operas made him a large fortune.

Schopenhauer

In 1854, Wagner read Arthur Schopenhauer's *The World as Will and Representation*, a long and difficult book about the nature of the world, the arts and the purpose of human life. The book had first been published in 1818 and ignored almost ever since. Wagner was immensely impressed by it and by the summer of 1855 had read it through four times. He never ceased to re-read it, to talk about it and to recommend it to others. Schopenhauer was the only thinker Wagner seemed to have any regard for as being an even greater genius than himself and he tried unsuccessfully to have a special professorship established at Zurich University for the study of Schopenhauer's philosophy.

Schopenhauer argued that music was more important than all the other arts. Music, unlike painting or sculpture or drama, which represent things or people, is abstract and can therefore represent the true reality which lies at the heart of the universe. This tied in very closely with Wagner's own ideas about the supremacy of music.

Schopenhauer also argued — as Buddhism does — that human life necessarily involves pointless pain and suffering and that death therefore represents a release. This view ties in with a constant theme in Wagner's operas in which love brings grief, and death resolves the situation.

Schopenhauer's ideas focused on problems of pain, beauty and human will, influencing Tolstoy as well as Wagner.

Success and Exile

In London, Wagner failed to make contact with Bulwer-Lytton, on whose story of *Rienzi* he was staking his future. Undaunted, he crossed to Boulogne where, by chance, the composer Meyerbeer happened to be staying. Meyerbeer generously listened to the libretto of *Rienzi* and gave Wagner letters of introduction to the director and conductor of the Paris Opera.

Despite this promising beginning, Wagner was not destined to succeed in Paris. In March 1840, *Das Liebesverbot* was accepted for performance but two months later, the theatre which had agreed to take it went bankrupt. *Rienzi* was completed in November 1840 and was accepted by the Dresden Court Theatre. Meanwhile Wagner had to take whatever work he could get to feed himself and his wife. He wrote orchestral arrangements, prepared vocal scores and reviewed the Paris music scene for a Dresden newspaper. It was not enough. The Wagners had **to pawn** their valuables and were then so desperate that they had to sell the pawn tickets. To save fuel they lived in just one room of their apartment. And all that time Wagner was working so hard he only allowed himself a break for a walk every fourth day. When he wasn't preparing scores, orchestrating or reviewing he devoted his remaining time and energy to sketching out ideas for more operas, most of which came to nothing at all.

More than two desperate years passed before Wagner and Minna left Paris in disgust and made their way to Dresden where preparations for the première of *Rienzi* were finally under way. When *Rienzi* was

FACSIMILE (THEATER PROGRAMME OF THE FIRST *RIENZI* PERFORMANCE).

The theatre programme for the first performance of *Rienzi* in 1842.

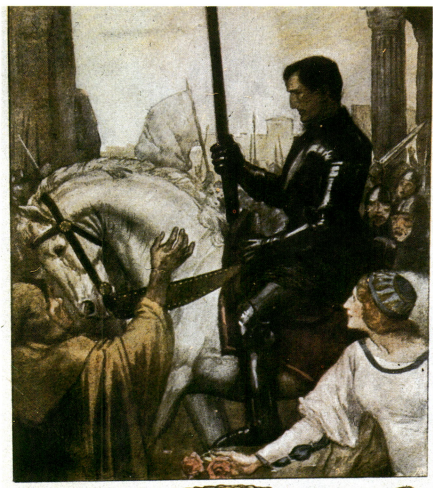

Rienzi — a noble and tragic figure — who foreshadows future Wagner heroes.

at last performed on 20 October 1842, it was an immense success. Apart from the music and the star performance of Wagner's long-time heroine Wilhelmine Schröder-Devrient, the audience warmed to the story itself, how the hero ends the corrupt rule of the aristocracy only to fall victim to conspiracy and his own ambition.

Wagner was quick to follow up his triumph with another work, *Der Fliegende Holländer (The Flying Dutchman)*. The inspiration for this had come partly from his own storm-tossed voyage aboard *Thetis* and partly from a legend re-told by a Parisian acquaintance, the

A contemporary picture of a dramatic moment from *The Flying Dutchman* (1843).

German poet Heinrich Heine. The story concerns a Dutch sea captain condemned to sail the seas forever unless he can win the true love of a woman. Written in Paris (where he had already sold the outline of the story once) it was premièred on 2 January 1843. Once again Schröder-Devrient had a leading role but, compared to *Rienzi*, *The Flying Dutchman*'s reception was lukewarm. Nevertheless a month later Wagner was offered, and accepted, the vacant post of joint Kapellmeister at the court of the King of Saxony.

As Kapellmeister, Wagner's responsibilities included supervising the music of the royal chapel, the opera and orchestral concerts and composing pieces for special court occasions. Wagner dutifully attended to these tasks but poured his creative energy into *Tannhäuser*, the first of his works to be based on medieval German mythology, which was to inspire almost everything he was to write in the future. *Tannhauser* had its première at Dresden on 19 October 1845. It did not go well. The scenery failed to arrive in time, and the lead tenor had laryngitis. The audience was unimpressed.

Wagner continued to take his official duties seriously and spent three months working on a report "Concerning the Royal Orchestra", which covered everything from the musicians' salaries and contracts to their seating arrangements. The composer's suggestions were sensible and practical and yet ignored. Wagner wanted to reward quality rather than seniority. His suggested reforms were, of course, a criticism of the existing system and its managers. His new ideas upset many people and would have upset even more if they had been carried out. After a year the report was officially rejected. Later Wagner came up with an even more revolutionary idea — that Saxony should take the lead in establishing a German national theatre. That project, too, remained a dream.

Wagner received a regular salary, though not a generous one, as Kapellmeister. Minna managed as best she could and enjoyed being the wife of a court official. But Wagner hated the pettiness of life in a provincial backwater and still dreamed of a career which would be filled with drama and greatness. He also continued to live far beyond his means, running up yet more debts.

Wagner's wish to shake up the Dresden music scene, to make a name for himself and to develop the idea of a German national theatre all led him towards an increasingly critical attitude to his royal employer and a corresponding sympathy for radical ideas. When a popular uprising broke out in May 1849, Wagner joined the cause. What he actually did is not quite clear but it was enough to make him flee into exile when the revolt collapsed.

Wagner went first to Weimar, where the pianist and composer

Tannhäuser, a story from German myth, as staged in Munich in 1867.

Revolutionaries at the barricades in Dresden in 1849. Wagner's role is uncertain.

Franz Liszt was preparing a production of *Tannhäuser*. After a brief stay in Paris he finally settled in Zurich where Minna at last and very reluctantly joined him. To her further despair Wagner turned away from writing even partly successful operas to grinding out long books on his theories about art. They were to be important and influential works, but, as Minna well knew, they would not pay the rent.

In his book, appropriately titled *Art and Revolution*, Wagner argued that art should not be the preserve of the privileged few but the expression of the genius of a whole people, hence his project for a German national theatre. In *The Art Work of the Future* he suggested that that genius of a people would best be expressed by a blend of music, poetry and dance, supported by painting, sculpture and architecture. Next came *Opera and Drama*, concerning Wagner's belief that musical drama should be built around the interweaving of distinctive themes (leitmotivs), each being associated with a major character to reveal their motivation and significance. During this period Wagner also wrote *Jewishness in Music*, a nasty attack on Meyerbeer, who had in fact done so much to give him work in Paris. Wagner had, however, convinced himself that all the while Meyerbeer had been conspiring to hold him back.

If anything was holding Wagner back, it was Wagner himself. Unable to return to Germany, he was unable to see *Lohengrin* when Liszt premièred it in Weimar — though he did manage to spend the royalties which it was supposed to bring but never did. To raise more cash, therefore, Wagner offered Liszt the rights to the first performance of the work which was to obsess him and become his masterpiece — a re-working of the medieval epic poem, the *Nibelungenlied*.

Wagner began with what was eventually to become the climax of the work — the story of the death of Siegfried, the perfect hero. He then realized that he needed to explain to his audience how this tragedy had come about, so he planned three more operas to precede it. The whole thing was to be called *The Ring of the Nibelung*. It would begin with *The Rhine Gold*, be developed through *The Valkryrie* and *Siegfried* and end with *Siegfried's Death*, which was later retitled *The Twilight of the Gods*. It was, to say the least, an immensely ambitious project, and to perform it as Wagner believed it should be presented would require a special theatre where all the required spectacle and effects could be provided. Wagner was not at all dismayed that he was unemployed, heavily in debt and in exile and threw himself into the task of composition. By 1852 he had sketched all four **libretti** and exhausted himself in the process.

In 1853, Wagner's admirers, led by a Zurich couple, the wealthy Wesendoncks, sponsored a festival entirely devoted to his music, much of which was to be performed for the first time. There followed a trip to Italy, where ideas for the music of *The Ring* began to flood in on him, and to Paris, where he called on Liszt and met the composer's 16-year-old daughter, Cosima. Returning to Zurich, Wagner made rapid progress with *The Rhine Gold* and *The Valkyrie* but had to fend off his creditors by signing over to Otto Wesendonck future performance rights to *Tannhäuser* and *Lohengrin* in return for cash. To make matters even more complicated, Wagner meanwhile had fallen in love with Wesendonck's wife, Mathilde.

In 1855, Wagner presided over another festival of his music and was invited to London by the

Franz Liszt (1811-86) was already the greatest pianist of his day by the age of 15.

Lohengrin confirmed Wagner's commitment to German myth as his main inspiration.

Philharmonic Society. He conducted eight concerts there, won the approval of Queen Victoria and met the French composer Hector Berlioz. In 1856, Wagner finished *The Valkyrie*.

By 1857, Wagner and his wife were residing in a lakeside cottage provided by the Wesendoncks, who lived next door. The composer was by now working on Act Two of *Siegfried*, the third of the four operas of *The Ring*. At that point, he put the whole project aside for the next 10 years, perhaps despairing of ever staging it, even if he did manage to complete it. Instead he turned to a quite new work, *Tristan and Isolde*, a story of hopeless love which mirrored his own relationship with Mathilde Wesendonck. By the spring of 1858, Minna had once again had enough and stormed off to Germany.

Wagner drifted to Venice and then back to Lucerne, where he finished *Tristan* in August 1859 and then set off for Paris, hoping that it could be staged there.

In Paris, Wagner gave a concert which the public loved as much as the critics hated it. He met the poet Baudelaire and passed a pleasant afternoon with the ageing composer Rossini. Whatever else had happened to Wagner he had lost none of his ability to charm and fascinate through the power of his intellect and the sheer force of his personality. But he appeared to be getting nowhere as far as a production went until suddenly the emperor, Napoleon III, ordered the Opera to put on, not *Tristan*, but *Tannhäuser*. To meet the requirements of the Paris stage Wagner had to make artistic compromises, having the libretto translated into French verse and writing in a ballet sequence. He also subjected the cast to 164 rehearsals, running up enormous expenses in his pursuit of artistic perfection. Disaster awaited him. Rowdy young members of the fashionable "Jockey Club", who usually turned up midway through any opera just in time to catch sight of the ballerinas' legs, decided to shout down the first performance. At the second and third they came armed with whistles. Wagner withdrew the production. The only comfort that he could draw from a second bitter Parisian experience was that, thanks partly to the intervention of Napoleon III, an **amnesty** now allowed him to revisit Germany.

Over the next few years Wagner worked on *The Master Singers of Nuremburg* and wandered through Europe, making guest conducting appearances, keeping company with various ladies and keeping just ahead of his creditors. By 1864 he was in Stuttgart, aged 51 and penniless. His dreams of greatness appeared more impossible than ever. He needed a miracle and that is precisely what he got.

Mathilde Wesendonck (1828-1902), one of many wealthy patrons fascinated by Wagner's talent and mercurial personality.

Ludwig II of Bavaria

Born in 1845, Ludwig (Louis) came to the throne of Bavaria before he had even finished his studies. At first he sided with Austria against Prussia in the struggle for supremacy over the German-speaking peoples. After defeat in the "Seven Weeks War" (1866) he changed sides and joined Prussia in its war against France in 1870-71. He supported the idea of a German empire under the Prussian **Kaiser** in return for special privileges for Bavaria but he soon wearied of politics and devoted most of his time to his personal passions — supporting Wagner and building extravagantly. In the latter he followed the example of his grandfather, Ludwig I, who had made Munich the artistic capital of Germany. At Herrenchiemsee between 1878-85 he built, but failed to complete, a copy of Versailles, while his earlier Linderhof castle (1869-78) was modelled on the Trianon. The most remarkable, Neuschwanstein, was a fairytale fantasy, perched on a **crag** and decorated with scenes from Wagner's operas.

On 10 June 1886, a panel of doctors declared the king insane and his uncle, Prince Luitpold, took over as regent. Three days later "Mad King Ludwig" drowned himself.

(Above) **Ludwig, aged 31, in the uniform of a cavalry officer.** (Left) **Neuschwanstein castle became a retreat in which the king could act out his obsessions with Wagner's music and the myths which inspired it.**

A Royal Rescue

In May 1864, Wagner found himself receiving a messenger from an 18 year old admirer who had just become King Ludwig II of Bavaria. A few days later, monarch and musician met. Wagner was showered with praise and money and provided with a lakeside villa. Ludwig offered to build the composer not only a theatre for the performance of his works but also to found a music academy and a newspaper to spread his artistic views. Apart from rescuing Wagner from obscure **penury**, Ludwig also allowed him to complicate his life yet further by accepting his recommendation that the brilliant conductor Hans von Bülow should be appointed to his staff. Bülow had married Liszt's daughter, Cosima, and within a short time of her arrival in Bavaria, Cosima was carrying Wagner's child. Isolde, born in April 1865, was, however, passed off as though Hans were indeed her father and everything was as it should be.

In June 1865, *Tristan* was given its first performance in Munich. Ludwig thought it was wonderful, the rest of the audience was less than overwhelmed. And, if Wagner's revolutionary new music was winning him few admirers, his visibly powerful influence over the young king made him even less popular. Some courtiers regarded him as a straightforward sponger, out to raid the state treasury for what he could get, but others saw him as a political meddler. When he wrote an article for the press calling for the replacement of certain key ministers, he provoked a crisis which forced the monarch to order him out of the kingdom. Wagner first made his way into southern France, where a telegram caught up with him and informed him of Minna's death. Then he returned to Switzerland to work

Wagner with Cosima — their relationships was close but far from tranquil.

again on *The Master Singers*. In the summer of 1866 Cosima came to join him, with her children but without her husband. Ludwig also came to join him, distraught at their separation. Wagner persuaded him to return to his throne and his duties, which he did in time to see Bavaria get soundly beaten for siding with Austria in its war against Prussia. This disaster did, however, at least enable him to follow up Wagner's advice and replace some of his chief ministers. Wagner may still have been kept out of the country but he was definitely a power behind the throne nonetheless. Ludwig, for his part, continued the hero worship and did indeed try to establish the promised music academy and the newspaper, the *Suddeutsche Presse*. Wagner's contributions to that journal, however, only served to stir up even more resentment at his influence. In February 1867, Cosima and Wagner had a second child, Eva. Bülow, wishing to avoid a scandal that might cause all three of them to lose Ludwig's very valuable favour, played along with the fiction that he and Cosima were still happily married. No one, it seemed, wanted to jeopardize the staging of *The Master Singers* which Wagner finished in October and which Bülow was to conduct.

The theme of *The Master Singers* — the holy stature of German art — perfectly expressed the rapidly awakening national pride which would unify the country into a great new European power within a few years. The première, on 21 June 1868, was a complete triumph, with Wagner presiding over it from the royal box. Once *The Master Singers*

Poster for the première of *The Master Singers of Nuremberg*.

Walther sings before the Mastersingers, a chance to display virtuoso skills, in a scene from *The Master Singers*.

had been staged, Wagner and Cosima no longer needed Bülow or the pretence of respectability. They left for a vacation in Italy. Cosima informed her husband that she now wanted a divorce. He agreed. Ludwig was appalled at the shamelessness of it all and wounded that he had been so deceived by his mentors. But, for the moment, they no longer needed him either. With Cosima now firmly by his side, Wagner resumed work on *The Ring*. In June 1869, Cosima bore their third child whom they appropriately decided to call Siegfried and Cosima and Wagner were finally married in July 1870.

Ludwig, meanwhile, decided to go his own artistic way and ordered Bülow to put on a performance of *Tristan* which Wagner forbade.

Worse still, Ludwig then went on to stage *The Rhine Gold* and *The Valkyrie*. Wagner had, of course, always intended that the four parts of *The Ring* should be staged under nobody's direction but his own, on successive nights and as a totality, not in bits and pieces and away from his control. He was, however, powerless to prevent the king from doing what he wanted, and the king also had a legal agreement on his side. Wagner put *Siegfried* to one side, incomplete for the present, and moved on to *The Twilight of the Gods*.

A French illustration of *The Ride of the Valkyries*, possibly the best-known passage from all Wagner's music.

In April 1871, Wagner and Cosima went to Berlin to see the new emperor, William I. On their way they stopped in Bayreuth to see if the theatre there would be suitable for staging *The Ring*. They decided that it would not do, but they liked the town enough to want to live there. They immediately began to make plans for a "Festspielhaus" worthy of *The Ring*. When they got to Berlin, they presented the project to the young pianist, Carl Tausig, whom Wagner had known since he was 16. Tausig agreed to set up a network of Wagner Societies to raise money for the project. Within a couple of months, however, Tausig was dead of **typhoid** at the tragically early age of 29.

Throughout 1871 and the spring of 1872, Wagner worked on completing *The Ring* cycle. On 22 May 1872, his 59th birthday, he laid the cornerstone of the new theatre. Ludwig sent good wishes but no cash. The Wagner Societies also proved slow in coming up with funds. The composer exhausted himself in fundraising, but to little effect. Then, out of the blue, in March 1874, Ludwig suddenly came up with a loan of 100,000 talers (German currency). A month later the Wagners moved into their new home "Wahnfried" (Peace from Illusion), where the composer put the finishing touches to *Twilight of the Gods*. *The Ring* was now

The Wagners' purpose-built home at Bayreuth was also their final resting place.

Bayreuth — The Festival Theatre specially designed by Wagner to stage *The Ring* cycle.

complete. The next task was to stage it.

Organizing the first performance of *The Ring* cycle was an immense and complex task. Enormous quantities of sheet music had to be prepared for the orchestra and singers who, in turn, had to be recruited and rehearsed. Sets and costumes had to be designed and made. And still there was the ongoing chore of raising yet more money while the walls of the new theatre gradually went up. The whole of 1875 passed by and it was not until August 1876 that dress rehearsals were at last finished.

The first public performance of *The Ring* took place on August 13 1876 in the newly-completed Festspielhaus. The audience included the Emperor of Germany, the Emperor of Brazil, a Russian Grand Duke and, of course, Ludwig himself. The reception was ecstatic though Wagner himself noted many flaws and failings. And when it was all over there remained a massive shortfall of 150,000 German marks to be paid off.

The Ring

A detailed summary of the plot of *The Ring* could run to a hundred pages. There are no less than 30 major characters. But the main theme is quite clear — the ring itself stands as a symbol of the evil that power can bring upon the world when unchecked by virtue or love.

In the first scene of *The Ring*, a wicked dwarf, Alberich, steals a golden treasure from the Rhine Maidens and forges it into a ring which will give the owner power to rule the world, providing he renounces love forever. The ring is stolen by the chief of the gods, Wotan, so Alberich curses the ring and everyone who ever owns it. The course of this curse runs through the rest of the cycle as the ring destroys the gods themselves and the hero, Siegfried. The drama closes with Brunnhilde, Siegfried's wife, flinging the ring back into the depths of the Rhine, thus freeing the world from its curse, before she seeks her own end on Siegfried's **funeral pyre**.

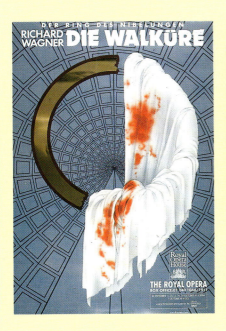
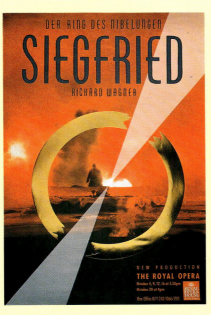

Posters for a modern version of *Siegfried* and *The Valkyrie*, the second and third parts of the four-part *Ring* cycle.

Last Years and Legacy

After the première of *The Ring*, Wagner took his family for a holiday in Italy to recuperate. Then it was back to face the debts arising from the performance. One way to pay off Wagner's debtors would be to allow other theatres to produce *The Ring* in return for a **royalty**. The problem with that, however, was that Ludwig insisted that only he had the rights to the work. Another way was to go back to conducting. An offer came from London — to conduct 20 concerts with the chance to earn £10,000. Unfortunately the theatrical agents were very inexperienced and their calculations were wildly inaccurate. When he arrived in London in April 1877, Wagner found that the Albert Hall would only be available for eight concerts, not 20. Furthermore, many of the best seats were privately owned and would therefore be occupied free.

Wagner had no option but to go ahead, though the strain on his health was by now becoming evident to his friends:

"Wagner did not do himself justice ... The rehearsals fatigued him and he was frequently faint in the evening. His memory played tricks on him and his beat was nervous."

In the end, even though the soloists agreed to accept a reduced fee, Wagner cleared only £700. A group of sympathetic Londoners added £500 more.

The financial clouds suddenly lifted in March 1878 when a new agreement was reached between the composer and his royal patron. Wagner agreed that Ludwig had the right to produce all his works at the Munich Court Theatre without payment. The King offered to set aside 10 per cent of all takings for Wagner performances in Munich and use them to pay off the outstanding debt of 98,000 German marks (Even so it took until 1906, 30 years after the first performance, to do this.)

Realising, perhaps, that his health was now seriously failing, Wagner decided to complete his last great creation, *Parsifal*, which was based on the legend of the Holy Grail. As winters became increasingly difficult for him to bear, he took to passing them in the warmth and sunshine of Italy and it was at Palermo, on the island of Sicily, that *Parsifal* was at last finished in January 1882. Ludwig agreed to back a production and the première took place on 26 July, when the Bayreuth Festspielhaus was re-opened for the first time since the performances of *The Ring* six years before. At Ludwig's insistence and against Wagner's opposition, the conductor was Hermann Levi, the son of a Jewish rabbi. Some might have seen it as merely ironic that the interpretation of a great Christian myth should be assigned to a Jew. Some may have seen no significance in

A scene from *Parsifal*, Wagner's last great work, showing the original scenery used in the Bayreuth production.

the matter either way. Wagner, however, saw it as a question of the deepest significance.

Although music was for Wagner the supreme art, he was a man of wide intellectual interests and a voracious reader of philosophy, history and religious texts throughout his life. He saw every aspect of his personal life as a question of moral or artistic significance. A vegetarian and a lifelong lover of animals, he was, for example, passionately opposed to **vivisection** and to meat-eating.

In the last five years of his life, Wagner resumed his literary career with vigour, dictating the completion of his autobiography to Cosima and, in the pages of the *Bayreuther Blätter*, a monthly journal which served as a newsletter of the Wagner Societies, working out a theory of culture which had a consistently anti-Jewish theme.

Asserting that Jews dominated the artistic scene, Wagner argued that they had taken over the German national heritage which, because they were not truly Germans, they could not truly represent. Wagner also attempted to separate Christianity from its roots in Judaism and suggested that Christ's own self-sacrifice on the cross was a dramatic gesture in favour of vegetarianism and against the spilling of blood.

In *Know Thyself* (1881), Wagner turned directly to the question of race, declaring that "pure" Germans were the noblest human form and calling for a renewal of their national awareness so that they could fulfil their historic destiny. Naturally Wagner looked to art rather than politics to achieve this. In *Siegfried* and *Parsifal* he had supplied models of moral perfection to be imitated.

Wagner was to die before Adolf Hitler was even born and it is doubtful whether the composer would have found the Nazis congenial company or convincing representatives of the pure German spirit. Nevertheless, it remains true that Hitler himself was a fanatical devotee of *The Ring* and an ardent supporter of the Bayreuth Festival. No doubt he could identify completely with the heroic Siegfried battling against the forces of evil. And his last days, besieged in his Berlin bunker, as he ordered the destruction of all Germany around him, show a striking parallel with the *Twilight of the Gods* which ends in fire and universal catastrophe.

Wagner's influence in the later course of German history can therefore easily obscure the scale of his artistic achievement. Generations of composers and writers have acknowledged their debt to him, both for his contribution to ideas about art and for his efforts in realising them. *The Ring*, which represents only a part of his immense output, is, after all, the largest single musical composition ever attempted by a single artist.

In September 1882, the Wagners returned to Italy, settling in Venice for the winter. On the morning of 13 February 1883, Cosima and the composer had a heated argument about the imminent arrival of a pretty young English singer. Wagner retired to his study to sulk and work on an essay. In the early afternoon he suffered a massive heart attack while sitting at his desk. Cosima rushed in in time for him to die in her arms. It was 24 hours before they could prise her

The funeral of Brunnhilde — a typical Wagner example of spectacle.

away from the body.

Wagner was buried, as he had planned, in the garden at Wahnfried. Cosima, supported by their son Siegfried, presided over the annual Bayreuth Festival for more than 30 years, fiercely guarding Wagner's artistic legacy. In 1930 she was laid to rest beside her husband.

Both in his writings and in his music, Wagner's purpose was to move his audience as powerfully as possible. And he did, long after his death, in ways perhaps that even he could never have imagined.

Find Out More...

Important Books

The New Grove: Wagner by John Deathridge and Carl Dahlhaus (Macmillan, 1984)

The Darker Side of Genius: Richard Wagner's Anti-Semitism by Jacob Katz (University Press of New England, 1986)

Wagner by Barry Millington (Vintage 1984)

The Real Wagner by Rudolph Sabor (Cardinal, 1987)

Richard and Cosima Wagner: Biography of a Marriage by Geoffrey Skelton (Gollancz, 1982)

Richard Wagner: His Life, Art and Thought by Ronald Taylor (Panther, 1983)

Important Addresses

University of Edinburgh
Collection of Historic Musical Instruments
Reid Concert Hall
Bristo Square
Edinburgh EG8 9AG

Finchcocks
Living Museum of Music
Goudhurst
Kent TN17 1HH

Royal College of Music
Museum of Instruments
Prince Consort Road
London SW7 2BS

The Bate Collection of Historical Instruments
Faculty of Music
University of Oxford
St. Aldate's
Oxford OX1 1DB

Important Dates

1813 Born in Leipzig
1814 Marriage of his mother to Ludwig Geyer
1820 Takes first piano lessons
1822 Goes to school
1828 Changes his surname from Geyer to Wagner
     Writes *Leubald*
1829 Writes first musical composition
1830 Leaves school, takes violin lessons and studies Beethoven
1831 Attends university
1832 His C major symphony is written and performed
1833 Becomes chorus master at Würzburg and writes *Die Feen (The Fairies)*
1834 Meets Minna Planer and makes debut as a conductor
1836 *Das Liebesverbot* performed
     Marries Minna
1837 Appointed musical director at Königsberg and Riga

1839 Flees Riga for Paris via London
1842 Leaves Paris
Successful première of *Rienzi*
1843 Première of *The Flying Dutchman*
Appointed Kapellmeister to the King of Saxony
1845 Première of *Tannhauser*
1849 Flees to Switzerland after failure of Dresden uprising
1850 Publishes *Jewishness in Music*
Liszt supervises première of *Lohengrin* in Weimar
1851 Finishes *Opera and Drama*
1853 Publishes complete poem of *The Ring*
Meets Cosima
1854 Affair with Mathilde Wesendonck begins
1855 Conducting in London
1857 Ceases work on *The Ring* cycle
1861 Disastrous performance of *Tannhauser* in Paris
1862 Breaks with Minna
1863 Stages concerts in Russia and central Europe
1864 Ludwig II becomes his patron and Cosima becomes his mistress
1865 Première of *Tristan*
Forced to leave Bavaria
1868 Première of *The Master Singers*
1869 Resumes composition of *The Ring*
1870 Marries Cosima
1872 Selects sites for Festspielhaus and Wahnfried
1874 Completes score on *The Ring* and moves to Wahnfried
1876 Première of the full *Ring* cycle
1877 Conducts concerts in London
1882 Première of *Parsifal*
Leaves for Venice
1883 Dies and is buried at Wahnfried

Glossary

Amnesty A general pardon.
Cantor The leader of the singing in a church.
Crag A rough, steep rock or cliff.
Funeral pyre A specially built "bonfire" upon which a dead body was burned.
Kaiser A German emperor.
Libretto (plural Libretti) The book of words (script) of an opera.
Myths Ancient traditional stories of gods or heroes.
Pawn, to To hand over personal possessions as security in exchange for money. A pawn ticket is issued and when this is finally handed back, along with the borrowed money, the goods will be returned.
Penury Great poverty.
Royalty Payment to a composer or author, etc. for every public performance or every copy sold.
Tenor The highest singing range in adult men.
Typhoid A feverish illness, at one time often fatal.
Vivisection The act of performing surgical operations on living animals for the purpose of research and experiments.

Index

Art and Revolution 14
Art Work of the Future, The 14

Bach 5
Ban on Love, The 7,10
Baudelaire 17
Bavaria 18
Bayreuth 22
Bayreuth Festival 28,29
Bayreuther Blätter 28
Beethoven 5,6
Berlioz, Hector 16
Bulwer-Lytton 8,10

Dresden 10
Dresden Uprising 13,14

Fairies, The 6
Feen, Die 6
"Festspielhaus" 22,24,26
Fidelio 5
Fliegende Holländer, Der 11
Flying Dutchman, The 11

Geyer, Cecilie 5
Geyer, Ludwig 4

Heine, Heinrich 12
Herrenchiemsee 18
Hitler, Adolf 28

Jewishness in Music 14
"Jockey Club" 17

Know Thyself 28

Leipzig 4,5,6
Leubald and Adelaide 4
Levi, Hermann 26
Liebesverbot, Das 7,10
Linderhof Castle 18
Liszt, Cosima 15,19,20,21,22,28,29
Liszt, Franz 14,15
Lohengrin 14,15,16
London Philharmonic Society 16
Ludwig II 18,19

Master Singers of Nuremburg, The 17,20,21
Measure for Measure 7
Meyerbeer, Giacomo 8,10,14
Munich Court Theatre 26

Napoleon III 17
Nazis 28
Neuschwanstein 18
Nibelungenlied 15

Opera and Drama 14

Parsifal 26,27,28
Planer, Amalie 8
Planer, Christine Wilhelmine (Minna) 7,8,10,13,14,16
Prince Constantin 4
Prince Luitpold 18

Queen Victoria 16

Rhine Gold, The 15,22
Rienzi 8,10,12
Ring of the Nibelung, The 15,16,21,22,23,24,25,26,28
Rossini 16

Schopenhauer, Arthur 9
Schröder-Devrient, Wilhelmine 5,10,12
Schumann 5
"Seven Weeks War" 18
Siegfried 15,16,22,28
Siegfried's Death 15
Suddeutsche Presse 20

Tannhäuser 12,13,14,15,17
Tausig, Carl 23
Tristan and Isolde 16,17,19,21
Twilight of the Gods, The 15,22,23,28

Valkryrie, The 15,16,22
Von Bülow, Hans 19,20,21

Wagner, Albert 4,5,6
Wagner, Johanna 4,5
Wagner, Karl Friedrich Wilhelm 4
Wagner, Richard
   Born in Leipzig 4
   Studies composition 5
   Becomes chorus-master 6
   Marries Minna Planer 8
   Première of *Rienzi* 10
   The Flying Dutchman 12
   Becomes joint Kapellmeister 12
   Writes books on theories about art 14
   Starts work on *The Ring* 15
   Birth of daughter, Isolde 19
   Death of Minna 19
   Birth of second child, Eva 20
   Marries Cosima Liszt 21
   First public performance of *The Ring* 24
   Dies 28
Wagner, Rosalie 4,6
Wagner, Siegfried 21,29
Wagner Societies 23,28
"Wahnfried" 23,29
Weber 4
Weinlig, C.T. 5
Wesendonck, Mathilde 15,16,17
Wesendonck, Otto 15,16
William I 22
World as Will and Representation, The 9

Picture Acknowledgements

The Publishers would like to thank the following for their kind permission to reproduce their photographs in this book: Mansell Collection 8,18(bottom),19,24; Mary Evans frontispiece, 10,11,12,13,14,15,16,20,21,22,23,27,29; Nationalarchiv der Richard Wagner Stiftung/Richard Wagner Gedenkstätte Bayreuth 5,7,9; Popperfoto 17,18(top); Royal College of Music cover; Royal Opera House 25; Zefa 6.